Between
Light and Shadow

Edda R Smith

BookLeaf
Publishing

Presentation by *BookLeaf Publishing*

Web: www.bookleafpub.com

E-mail: info@bookleafpub.com

ISBN: 9789357691833

First edition 2022

To Alex who supports me and pushes me to follow my dreams, always.

And to Robert for all our deep and mad conversations late at night.

Poems

Monsters

Sometimes the monsters I am more afraid of
lay within me.

They sleep lightly and can wake up
at any moment.

One of my worst fears is that one day
they will take over my mind,
forcing my other self to leave.

Will that be the end of me
or a new beginning?

The Rain

2

The sound of rain
washes off the sorrow of the day.
It comforts me; it cleanses me.

A part of me wants to drown in the water, finally
silencing the pain
that loudly screams my name.

A part of me wants to allow death to purge me, to
ease all burdens,
until the silent echo of a memory remains,
and water is all that's left of me.

When Depression Comes

3

While lying peacefully
in the clear blue water of the ocean,
a sudden sense of doom takes over my mind.

The water turns into mud,
clogging my body, choking me.
I am trapped; I cannot escape.

I lay still,
waiting for my depression to grow tired of me.
I hold on,
although every cell in my body begs me
to let go.

One question echoes in my head:
'Is this worth it?'

Glimpse

I am afraid to look into your eyes,
yet yearn for every drop of blue they offer.

I look at you when you can't see me.
Sometimes, when I study your smile,
I catch a glimpse of sadness.

Why do you hide it?
I feel your darkness and welcome it.
You matter to me.

I accept you and love you.
Why can't you see that?
Why do you push me away?

Limbo

5

I am in limbo
between reality and imagination.
I miss moments that never existed.

I miss your lips on my neck,
your arms around me,
the warmth of your body against mine.

I miss your hand gently caressing my cheek
before kissing me;
I miss you whispering in my ear that everything
will be ok.

I miss you so much it hurts,
and yet my mind cannot comprehend
how I can miss something I never had.

Lost Smile

I search for a fragment of your smile,
but it is not there.

Maybe it is hidden under piles of pain,
debris and dust.

The life you had is now lost into the abyss,
and so are your dreams.

How can I find you in the darkness
when I am lost myself?

Loud Silence

And yet it's the silence
I cannot stop listening to.

It's loud, intrusive, possessive.
The missing words, the absence of warmth.

Did I imagine it?

For a brief yet eternal moment,
I saw a different reality.
Is that reality that made your voice hush?

Perhaps it was a dream,
but I was the only conscious person.

Encounter with Mother Death

I saw Mother Death today
She looked deeply into my eyes
    "It's a mistake!" I tried to say
    "I'm not ready to say my goodbyes."

A sharp pain touched my heart.
I thought about everything I'd lose.
    "It's too early for my depart."
She looked at me, confused.

    "I thought this was what you wanted",
she whispered
But when I looked to my left,
pain struck my heart again.
I saw the man I loved crying by my bed
 Looking back into her eyes, I said,
    "Please give me a chance to explain."

"I'll fight for him until my last breath."
A gentle smile appeared on her face.
    "I beg you not to take me away today,
    Mother Death."
She then touched my face with peculiar grace.

"It won't be your day today,
But look deep into my eyes
Because next time you'll see them
nothing you will say
will stop you from meeting your demise."

The Mould

I thought I needed to make myself small
not to scare you away.

I watered down my character,
hid my knowledge,
forgot any talent I had.

So I became a shadow, a ghost.
I cut myself into small pieces
to fit the Mould you had prepared for me.

Only the Mould was a coffin,
and I already helped you dig the grave for it.

Worth Ignoring

As painful as twenty-one arrows striking my
thorax, your silence fills the halls of my mind.

I am furious with myself for allowing you to play
with me.
I question my worth every silent second you are
not here.

Who am I? A huntress or a prey?
Am I part of someone's imagination?
I gave meaning to our quiet conversations
as if you planned to harm me.

In truth, I do not exist in your world.
I am not even worth ignoring.

God was a Line

God was a line,
>that line between the wall and the ceiling.
I looked at that line whilst praying.
I asked for forgiveness, confessing all my sins in
the darkness.
>No one ever responded.

God was a line,
>that line that separates the sky and the sea
>on the horizon.
I looked at that line whilst being pinned down by
a man older than me who demanded something I
wasn't willing to give.
>No one was there.

 God was a line,
>that line between marble tiles on the
>Sicilian floor.
I looked at that line while being hit and kicked
because I dared to speak.
>No one heard me.

 God was a line,

   that line on my forearm I traced with a
   razor one time I couldn't handle life
   anymore.
I looked at that line spilling precious red fluid
and wondered how much longer I needed to wait.
          No one held me.

God was a line,
   that line on the screen of an ECG
   machine.
A flat line.
God doesn't have a heartbeat.
          God is dead.

Attention Seeking

What if we replace attention-seeking
with support-seeking?

Would that change the
way the world sees us?

Would that change the way you see yourself?

Colourblind

The colours are not the same.
They are dull, uncomfortably still.
Lifeless, as if the world around me wants to
match my core.

I yearn for some colour like a starving child who
craves his mother's milk.
I am a painter and can only use washed-up grey
to illustrate the rainbow.

Red is the only colour I can find.
It exists in pain, music, and blood.
So I hurt myself while listening to some tragic
violin concerto, looking at the blood slowly
dripping down my fingers.

That's how I know I am not colourblind.
That's how I know I am not dead.

Piece by Piece

I sacrificed my boundaries for the people I loved
and that swiftly brought chaos into my life.

By doing right for them, I abandoned myself and
betrayed my spirit.
Piece by piece, I gave away parts of me that I'll
never get back.
Fragments of my whole self that I needed to
regrow.

My time, my integrity, my beliefs, my memories.
Only some things could be replaced or recreated.
Certain things just vanished.
They are lost forever, perhaps, but in my mind,
they are unforgotten.

Shipwreck

There is always beauty and sadness
surrounding a shipwreck.
I like to imagine what that ship looked like
before being doomed to be forsaken and
forgotten.

I imagine the plans, the colours, the passengers.
The hopes, dreams and desires of people
inhabiting it.

It reminds me of a child
with a future as bright as the sun
before being hit by the harsh reality of life.

I imagine the sea hitting the ship
over and over again,
eroding it until, eventually,
there will be nothing left of it.

We are the child; we are the shipwreck.

Three

Three
like the times you tried to end your life.
This life was too much for you,
and you just wanted to fly away.

Three
like the times I hugged you last time I saw you.
I knew it was our last time together
and I couldn't let you go.

Three
like the times I broke down
on my way to the airport,
knowing I would never see you again.

Lucid Dreaming

Sometimes I need to pause my dreams.

Dissect them, rewind them and start again.

My nightmares become chess matches with myself,
yet somehow I always lose.

Forever

How can I promise you forever?
I never believed in it.
I believe that people change, evolve,
succumb to their own nature.

Sometimes forever is not long enough...
Sometimes it is too long, and I need to break free.
I was forced to promise forever to two people
before, and I broke that oath twice.

What does that make me?

I believe in now. I believe in my feelings,
in my body, in this exact moment.
I cannot vouch for the future.
All I have is the present, and that's enough for
me.

Stay

"Don't think that! Stay for me," they say.
What a clumsy way of love they portray.

"Stay for your dreams, your family,
and anything else that matters."
and with their words,
my hope for this pain to end shatters.

Even so, I stay another day and then one more
because, as always,
I put somebody else's needs before my own.

All I need to do is to take another deep breath.
They don't realise that living is harder than
succumbing to death.

So I lay here,
waiting for Mother Death to arrive,
to take me in her arms and say that
it's now my time.

Light and Shadow

Between Light and Shadow
my soul is divided.

Not entirely black
nor completely white.

Only by exploring both paths
we'll know which one to take.

It was the beginning of my demise when I realised
that this was the only way to live life.

So I sinned; I dragged my soul
into the mud, and I realised that
my search for truth had only just begun.

Between Light and Shadow,
my soul will always be divided.

www.ingramcontent.com/pod-product-compliance
Lightning Source LLC
LaVergne TN
LVHW010853200726
843508LV00012B/2889